Of birds I know that they have wings to fly,
of fish that they have fins to swim,
and of wild beasts that they have feet to run.
Yet who knows how dragons hurdle clouds and
rise to heaven?
This day I have met Lao Tzu and he is a dragon.

attributed to Confucius

© 2020
Peaceful Dragon Press

Lao Tzu

The Way

**an interpretation
by David Marks**

DEAR MERRITT,
THANKS FOR YOUR EFFORTS
TO BRING MORE LIGHT
TO THE WORLD.
KINDEST REGARDS,
David

Preface

This previously unpublished poetic version of Lao Tzu's *Tao Te Ching* was written in 1976. Upon its completion, it served as a thesis in my final year at the *International College of Oriental Medicine* in England.

Although many of my classmates wrote compelling papers on various treatments of disease with acupuncture, I chose a philosophical topic, as this was more applicable to how I would approach my future pursuits.

Having studied Chinese philosophy at university, including a course on the *Tao Te Ching*, I found the wisdom in this text presented a fascinating premise for the cause of discord and disease. Interpreting Lao Tzu's verses deepened this understanding and supplied a foundation for my continuing exploration into Traditional Chinese Medicine.

Lao Tzu's insightful perspective demonstrates how suffering people often don't recognize their place in the natural world. He describes how awareness of the ways of nature can support contentment and well-being.

This new edition, considerably revised with the application of further understanding and experience to the text, focuses on expressing the concepts of Lao Tzu so that they might be understood and appreciated by people from all walks of life.

★★★

Introduction

Over centuries, Lao Tzu's *Tao Te Ching* has been translated and adapted hundreds of times. Through its subtle wisdom and timeless appeal, its message has endured and continues to inspire readers.

There is no definitive edition of the *Tao Te Ching* in any language. To begin to understand a Chinese philosophical treatise that is nearly 2500 years old, some subjective interpretation is required.

Tao Te literally translates as *the way of the virtuous*. *Ching* is a classic work, but as with the contents, the title's meaning is open to some interpretation. This version is simply titled, *The Way*, as the broader concept of the *Way* or *Tao* incorporates remaining in harmony with the natural order of life.

Mystics, students and teachers have discussed the meaning and application of Lao Tzu's text since its first appearance. Its origin also remains the subject of fables and scholarly debate.

The first known copies of the *Tao Te Ching* date from the fourth century B.C., and were written on strips of bamboo. Lao Tzu, meaning *old master*, is said to have lived sometime before then, as early as the sixth century B.C. Some historians have characterized him as a legendary figure, though the name may refer to a number of different people who lived over several hundred years. This is something we can never know for sure.

For the purposes of this version, imagine Lao Tzu was a humble, wise and respected person who never sought fame or fortune. Legend describes how, as an elderly man, Lao Tzu reluctantly encapsulated his profound intuitive views and practical thoughts into a single, short poetic essay.

According to recent research, the *Tao Te Ching* was inspired by *The Yellow Emperor's Classic of Internal Medicine*, the first treatise on the philosophical and practical elements of Traditional Chinese Medicine.

Both texts advise on how to remain in a balanced state and prevent disorder. Although there is no confirmed date of the appearance of *The Yellow Emperor's Classic of Internal Medicine*, there is general agreement that it predates the time of Lao Tzu.

Regardless of its origins, the *Tao Te Ching* remains one of the most ancient, profound and important commentaries on the human condition.

With its metaphysical concepts set out in a short form of eighty-one verses, Lao Tzu's philosophy has invited numerous contrasting translations and interpretations. Because Classical Chinese characters represent words or concepts, and can only be understood within their specific context, even the most literal versions attribute different meanings to the original Chinese text.

Some have claimed that one edition or another, whether literal or interpretive, stands out above others; this is the subject of ongoing debate. Nonetheless, every translation contains some essence of the text's original meaning, and Lao Tzu's perspective shines through.

The original Chinese *Tao Te Ching* has poetic verses that add emphasis to the meaning and make the stanzas easier to memorize and share. The overall editorial approach to this new version attempts to do the same, making the concepts understandable to the reader by finding the essence of the original text within a rhythmic structure. The rhyming stanzas clarify themes and enhance their meaning. And, as in the original Chinese text, the poetic format allows for easier recollection.

The Way is extrapolated from early 20th century English translations of the *Tao Te Ching*, commentaries on the original Chinese text and an understanding of the basic tenets of Traditional Chinese Medicine. These elements serve as the foundation and words chosen for this version.

Lao Tzu begins by describing the weakness of words in understanding the natural order. It would defy any logic that his treatise would go on to explain nature with complex, obscure descriptions.

Thus an overt, reductionist approach has been applied here that distills both concepts and terms. This *Tao Te Ching*, when compared to others, may be deemed simplified or imprecise relative to the original characters or their place in the stanzas. Though an understandable critique, for most readers, *The Way* will present the concepts in a lucid and accessible form, true to the meaning and intent of the original.

The word nature or creation is used to understand *Tao*, where other versions might not translate this concept into English. *Tao* encompasses a natural, unknown, pervasive force; nature and creation are applied similarly with their broadest definition: the manifestation of an omnipresent power within and without us.

Lao Tzu also uses the terms in Chinese for heaven and earth, and they are occasionally used here because in context they add perspective to the central theme of universal creativity.

These cosmological concepts can be understood within a simple framework. Heavenly energy can be appreciated as air and sunlight, and earthly energy as food and material sustenance. In this view, all life, including human existence, is supported by a continuing cyclical process.

Traditional Chinese science rests on a unification theory that considers the perpetual flow of energy between *yin* and *yang*: terms used for passive and active elements. Heaven and earth represent these energies, with human life thriving between them.

Although Lao Tzu presents these concepts as foundational, the practicality of the *Tao Te Ching* comes from his application of cosmology to understanding internal and external human conflicts, decision making and leadership.

Lao Tzu's perspective on good leaders is not necessarily political. It can also be interpreted generally as a template for an individual's influence on harmonious social order.

A mystical text that emphasizes simplicity, *The Way* has unique effects and can take on different meanings as the reader's life circumstances change. It is not necessarily read in its entirety at once; individual chapters offer insights that readily stand alone.

The Way presents a world view that corresponds with the essential foundations of many spiritual and philosophical teachings. With its emphasis on humility and compassion as elements for improving the quality of life, it is also one of the most ancient and enduring guides to balanced living.

There is universal agreement that the original text encourages contemplation, and this version is certainly open to further interpretation and application, inviting readers to explore their own reactions to the concepts.

Through the veil of language, Lao Tzu's message remains clear. Understanding our place in the natural order is integral to establishing our equanimity and good health, and by extension, creating a better world for everyone.

★★★

Nature is a ceaseless force
indescribable with any word
its power essentially limitless
beyond what's seen and heard.

Language came only after
what made life come to be
the simple and the complex
defy terminology.

Words often separate
what is really the same
things appearing different
because of term or name.

This never-ending paradox
known since our tender youth:
at the heart of every wonder
is a wordless, simple truth.

To deem a thing beautiful
requires something to compare
praising apparent goodness
of the depraved you are aware,
life and death's causalities continue endlessly
difficult and easy are complementary,
high and low are often degrees of the same thing
long and short relate with constant contrasting,
the changing pitch of tones, give voice its quality
present is the past, when the future comes to be.

Thus to be natural
is to move as nature does,
to gently, quietly accept what is
and understand what was.

Work with joyful humility
when finished find your rest,
not competing in living
your competence is best.

To praise or detest brings quick unrest
causing others to contend
having more than most brings protest
the poor you will offend.

If displays of the self were to cease
all hearts and minds would be at peace.

Thus a good ruler is gentle and clear
feeding the hungry, maintaining good cheer
calming desires and firm as a bone,
nature's strength is simply shown
as a leader should be quietly known.

The universe is the mother of itself
the ancient source of nature's wealth
all that is sharp it smooths and wears
untangling knots and mending tears,
tempering the sun with a cooling breeze
calming storms with constant ease
infinitely powerful, always present,
its source a mysterious, timeless event.

Creation has no preference or care
it has no dogma, nor is self-aware,
a model for people to attain and see
through life and death, the spirit is free.

Nature breathes with constant change
yielding, it will rearrange
so vast in its realms
all free to enter
calm overwhelms
at its center.

Valleys never know breathlessness
they endure like a mother's tenderness,
their fertility, the source of everything
purely and quietly sustaining
effortlessly producing and prospering.

Nature forever expands and endures
infinitely vast, embracing all cures.

Thus a sound person from greed detaches
a selfish thought, stops and catches
remaining humbly happily behind
keeping simple peace of mind
pursuing kind and selfless deeds
fulfills a quest that has no needs.

Like water, we could effortlessly bring
natural fulfillment to everything,
streaming closely to the land
flowing as we understand
running gently and sincerely
visibly bright and clearly
without effort, always just
cooling the earth and settling dust
riding the current with consciousness
coursing and brimming with blamelessness.

Remain strong but light
don't look to have all
without giant leaps
it's less likely you'll fall.

An oft' sharpened knife
loses its blade
joy comes not with strife
or vast fortunes made.

Disappointment forever clings
to those attached to thoughts and things,
as nature does not contend or compete
find each moment already complete.

Leading your life individually
do you embrace eternity?

As a baby born breathes fresh air
can you awaken to the wholeness we share?

Cleanse your mind of guilt and fear
hold nature's precious essence dear
use your heart to guide and steer
toward all that's noble, simple and clear.

Nature breeds life and liveliness
nurturing without possessiveness
guiding without forcefulness
creating everything we bless.

Many spokes make a wheel
the space between is just as real
a clay pot is formed around
an emptiness thus made profound
doors and windows create a space
engendering a functional place.

The seed of all that was or is
remains an infinite source
that simply gives.

Dazzling beauty can leave us blind
a deafening sound can dull the mind
over-spiced food, its taste you'll not find.

Competing for profit drives people insane
lost or found, there's nothing to gain.

Know the sum of all parts
see both the forest and the trees,
the wise feel with their hearts
with their spirits at ease.

Fame and infamy are quite the same
people suffer with themselves to blame
the higher acclaim, the more likely the shame
self-obsession turns people insane.

Those who care for souls undone
move closer to the world as one
giving love and sharing more
they understand what life is for.

Look with nothing to see
hear where no sound can be
grasp without the need to feel
know that there's nothing unreal.

When unknowns are combined
something exists undefined
untangling all that appears to bind.

When darkness eclipses everything
a golden dawn can suddenly spring,
giving form and substance
from nothing it can come
perpetual, boundless,
meaningless to some.

This ancient potential, forever known
has no end and no beginning,
with ceaseless power and the clearest tone
creation keeps on winning.

In the distant past was a wisdom deep
misunderstood, too simple to keep,
some sayings endure, for they are not obscure:
crossing an icy stream
stay focused, don't dream,
when in danger, stay alert
a foolish mistake will get you hurt.

Constantly considerate? Here's the test:
do you always behave like a humble guest?

Desire is an illusion felt
like a piece of ice, about to melt
life's secrets have no key or lock
we are simply an un-carved block.

An empty valley with fertile pull
exemplifies what's really full.

Both the wise one and the fool
see something in a muddy pool
the fool stirs it up and more mud creates
the water clears as the wise one waits.

Flowing with life is enough
even when the water is rough
find gentle strength, you don't need to be tough.

Humility yields eternal peace
causing vitality to increase
a void fills, discord will then cease.

Return to the tranquility of breath
serenely accept both life and death.

Nature's path we should abide
though many fools have often tried
from creativity we cannot hide.

Seeing this way opens the mind
freeing the heart, peace we soon find,
then acting most majestically
feeling much more heavenly
aware of life's eternity,
we embrace nature's immortality.

Great rulers find strength
in the shadows and stay
where they don't demand
that people obey,
some foolish commanders
insist only they
should be highly honored
with tributes and pay,
tyrannical rulers
take basic rights away
leading to suffering
and freedom's delay,
the humblest leader
shows the most powerful way:
when work is done
the people say
we do this ourselves
for the love of each day.

When nature's silent way is lost
come rules and morals in its place,
decrees then kept at any cost
cause the loss of truth without a trace.

When a child and parent disagree
come calls for filial piety,
when corruption rules and people toil
leaders declare all must be loyal.

Wisdom can surely set you free
though a joyful life has a special key:
kindness is the source of liberty.

Reverence can become a habit
respect arrives only when you have it.

Thievery, greed and bold excess
breed a life with empty cleverness,
destructive and foolish, avarice goes on
the simpler way seems to be gone.

To reclaim all that's natural and free
begin with sincere humility.

Worries in life come from habits learned
with appraisals and value, be less concerned
from the distraction of madness, we can be turned
where ebb and flow can be discerned
brooding and worry must be spurned
if inner peace is deeply yearned.

The fool who does nothing, with a mysterious grin
has no one to turn to, nothing to win,
innocence rules, each day is clear
yet critics continue to chide and jeer
drifting through life, like a rogue wave at sea
roaming with simplicity,
others find battles lost or won
the fool wisely laughs
with nothing much done
at nature's bosom
in the glow of the sun.

The world manifests oneness
without need to explain
though each individual thing is given a name
seeming to divide the earthly plane.

Endlessly empty with eternal strength
ever-present in its boundless length:
the source of infinite creativity
has absolute singularity.

Yielding you need not break
bend for flexibility's sake,
empty, you take in all
lying down you won't fall,
profits cloud and confuse
without owning, there's nothing to lose.

The wise go on in this transparent way
embodying what all should display:
present, without showing
without justifying, knowing
never bragging, yet trusted and polite
not competing, with no need to fight.

Yielding you need not break,
so very clear, so true
life is a simple treasure
for all who take this view.

Nature doesn't insist on having its way
the wind can blow for half a day
it might rain all night and through the morning
then the sun could shine without warning,
creation need not be exact
what's seen as flawed has nothing lacked.

Within the way of life is found
a sense of being on the ground
but if nature's way is lost you'll see
a world without its gravity.

At one with all we feel at home
never with the sense of being alone,
while respect flows directionless
soothing pain and ending distress,
yet fail to honor all under the sun
and you'll not be honored by anyone.

Standing on tip-toes might cause you to fall
run too fast, soon you won't run at all,
touting your glory, unseen you remain
self-righteous behavior dishonors your name,
boasting won't replace that which you lack
pride is the sign of a directionless tack.

Simply follow nature's way
avoid extremes without delay
for living large invokes decay.

Within the birth of all that exists
from earth's deep core to heaven's light mists
a great single spirit simply persists
a changeless presence that never insists.

The universe is in reality
like a unified husband and wife
entwined in singularity
defining the way of life.

Passive and pervasive, flowing free
the source of all vitality
effortlessly circling back
within an endless spiraling track.

The way revolves around and through
each and every part
the universe encourages you
to keep creativity at heart,
following the way of heaven and earth
mirroring yang and yin
a glowing, timeless, flawless birth
without and deep within.

Grace emerges naturally
from a conscious focused will
like a great tree's stable roots
that keep the trunk firm and still.

A traveler on the road
thinks not of pressing needs
for calmness is the code
that guides both words and deeds.

There may be a thousand chariots
though you can only ride but one
abandon serene restraint
and reach oblivion.

A good pilgrim leaves nothing behind
the clear speaker has a sharp mind,
without tools or words spoken
one can add and subtract
or close what is open
with an instinctive act
and even squeezing most tightly
no one could extract
the essence which lightly
keeps all things intact,
thus abandoning nothing
caring for all
finding light in the dark
no matter how small,
seeing no one as strange
including those who are bad
understanding things change
finding joy in the sad
brings understanding
of what makes us glad,
to be honest and true
there's nothing else to do
so make sure your heart is unclad.

Passive and active
though opposing they are
are composites together
seen close or from afar.

There is no breach of wholeness
just illusory scars
light won't be broken
from the sun or the stars.

Creation has a natural state
seeming firmly to exist
then effortlessly shifts its shape
as water turns to mist.

Oneness pervades without limit
thus the sage always brings
a serene, humble spirit
feeling the unity of all things.

Nature's way cannot be changed
the sacred can't be rearranged,
attempts to mold it cause only harm
holding tight, you break the charm.

There is a time to move ahead
and a time to stay behind,
within the aspects of all life
strength and frailty you will find.

Some moments we breathe gently
sometimes catching a breath is hard
on most occasions we give freely
though at times we must be on guard:
wary of waste and blind excess
and the entanglements of elaborateness.

In keeping balance and peace profound
impediments are surely found
but fierce response as a standard course
only proves the futility of using force,
nothing good comes from showing strength
it only adds to trouble's length,
when heated discourse is unfolding
emotions you should be withholding.

Resist pride and avoid seeking glory
gently tell your simple story,
responses come more naturally
when avoiding negativity.

Rising fiery anger
only brings you harm,
to solve a problem simply
approach it without alarm.

Weaponry and violence are never for the good
though this simple logic is rarely understood,
foolish wars will take away
the peacefulness of a perfect day,
it's always the last unwelcome choice
to raise our hands or our voice
against aggressors who blindly come
upending balance for everyone.

The best of times are when motives are pure
saddest when greedy leaders endure,
a tyrant reviles in victory
the peaceful triumph in humility.

Nature is endless
pervading all
though some may profess
its importance is small.

If nature's laws are heeded
no further rules are needed,
chasms bridged
peace envisaged
like a spring rain
soothing pain
reviving all that is sane.

When the world appears divided
struggling with much undecided,
end all strife and thought pollution
with a clear and wise solution:
life can simply, calmly be
like a rolling river, flowing to the sea.

The intelligent might see details of something
the wise also know themselves,
the clever force change and trouble they bring
the patient one inwardly delves.

Satisfaction is so fleeting
with desires you're not free,
if expectations you're not meeting
find endless inherent stability.

Creativity fills the universe
blossoming in every way
always gentle, never terse
unlimited every day.

Replenishing, without making claim
seemingly without an aim,
with nothing to impose
or worship or endorse
that which flows and grows
from this nameless endless source.

When harmony is fulfilling life
we hear a single tone,
feeling everything as a oneness
knowing we never are alone.

Complex melodies may satisfy
and comforts sometimes call,
but it's an unmeasured, silent way
that brings together one and all.

Those feeling dark and down
once were very pleased
complaining with a dismal frown
that their joyfulness was seized.

The saddened and humiliated
once were feeling proud
if riches were expropriated
with wealth you were endowed.

Seeing this, the sane are sure
that not to strive is to endure,
as fish thrive in water clear and deep
by having less, the wise gently reap.

Harmony with nature
is the way of life,
selflessness emerges
free from any strife.
Inner calm precedes the times
when everything goes well,
no need to wander aimlessly
nor firestorms to quell.

Returning to simple serenity
nothing is desired,
through calm, detached, tranquility
peace is thus inspired.

Good people don't need to plan their goodness
yet they remain quite good
not striving, rather flowing, doing all they could
to find the joy in getting work done
while others struggle, adding up what they've won.

The kind don't think of kindness
nor favor being returned,
while those with fiery, greedy blindness
find themselves thus burned.

Restraining others from their passion
rarely will succeed
forcing their direction
won't keep them from their need,
when the natural way is lost
people flail, their kindness tossed
feigning goodness at any cost.

Arbitrary justice is something to ignore
when following nature's way
and creativity's basic lore
see that truth and fairness
comes from one's deep core
not caring for the reasons
others are changing for:
without judgment, there is no stress
simply have a no or yes.

The oneness of life complete in each part
clear like heaven with no end or start
a pervasive force felt in your heart.

No one can attempt to assault
nor disparage, nor find fault
the beauty within nature's deep vault.

If not for clarity, heaven would cloud
with stable firmness, earth is endowed,
if not for stamina, strength would stumble
if not for openness, valleys would crumble
from an infinite source continues all
without nature's endurance, all would fall.

Roots are required for creation
for every woman, man and nation
all things decay in stagnation
without a deep, secure foundation.

In realms high and low
where arrogance is first
all devolve and reflect the worst,
though sparkling and lovely
are diamonds and jade
from humble strong stone
great mountains are made.

Nature's constant cyclical stream
overcomes as we surrender to a heavenly dream,
this breath pervading all creation
is the elemental essence of all sensation.

The wise who sense the greater way
respect its path and its maxims obey,
some emulate this but cannot stay
and lose themselves in half a day,
a buffoon will laugh and always stray
from the solemn vows of yesterday.

Some are sure that nature's bright light
has never been kindled,
concerned with their own plight
claiming purity has dwindled,
that the world is deeply scarred
and that a pure quiet life is complex and hard,
that simplicity is an unworthy goal
in a broken complex world,
that nature is something to control
with its bounty to be unfurled,
they dwell in these dark haunts
sure of every twisted word,
while the sensible sage never flaunts
and needs not be seen or heard,
trusting the way, ignoring the taunts
with life's harmony preferred.

The oneness of all encompasses three,
heaven, earth and humanity,
day into night and night into day
creation's fullness knows no other way.

Our great fear is to be without
the things we've always had about
and those who thrive never doubt
others have more and they are left out.

The greedy are empty
but the generous we find
are fulfilled throughout life
with a satisfied mind.

Over and over we hear it said
gain too much and your soul is dead,
indeed this is great wisdom
that should remain in your head.

The gentle easily adapt
to a hard or difficult time
neither burdened nor entrapped
with a feeling most sublime
as within creation they are wrapped
in harmony and rhyme.

This peaceful path
is a simple scheme
yet for most people
it is only a dream.

Your life means more than compliments say
for important things, tribute cannot pay,
profits can bring hardship, to lose is to be light,
weighted by attachments is the saddest plight,
retaining too much surely ensures
losing it all, as nothing endures,
recognize how little is needed at the start
and peace and vitality will never part.

Looking for an end will never get one far
as all things continue, simple as they are,
constantly filling, though never drained
essentially reserved, yet unrestrained
straight as an arrow, with a beautiful curve:
embracing enigma, you'll find what you deserve.

As motion overcomes a chill
warmth does end when all is still
knowing this, you always will
face only tasks you can fulfill.

When nature's way is calmly heeded
everything appears that's needed
when the way is ignored
pain in life is underscored.

Great loss comes from great desire
discontent fuels longing's fire
those obsessed with selfish greed
should seek only what they truly need
excessiveness brings only trouble
with less and less your joy will double.

Experience helps us to condense
and understand, it makes more sense
to see the essence of life at your core
the heart of what you're searching for
without outward trappings to explore
find contentment within
and your spirit will soar.

Too much detail and finesse
burdens the heart and the mind,
living with less, ends all distress
and makes one clear and refined.

Less work to be done
less pain to overcome
that which causes lesser strain
leaves much less to explain.

Following the simple, natural way
ensures a calm and peaceful day.

The wisest are the kindest, as well
putting others before them, their heads never swell,
finding goodness in the good
and goodness in the bad
without limitation, making all people feel glad.

Faith in those
worthy of trust
and trusting the foolish
for this is a must,
as doubters may claim
that this can't be right
yet the humble should always
be searching for light.

Knowledge can't insist
or solve every plight
so trust like a child
to sharpen one's sight.

There are those tempting death
and some who love life
and others who endlessly
cause war and strife.

Countless reasons are given
by most everyone
to not follow the seasons
the moon and the sun,
yet there are a few
whose path is so true
that wild beast nor raging battle
can change their course, nor spirit rattle
by claw nor blade, never harmed
the truly peaceful are not alarmed
never finding themselves disarmed.

A ceaseless existence
gives rise to all things
breath feeds life
and essential energy brings,
without insistence or force
nature differentiates the course
without need to endorse
nor wish to show
nor let all know
supporting all that will grow
from the high to the low.

Oneness is the source of all that will be
awareness of this truth ensures that we're free
the eyes can look, the mind will see.

Remaining within yourself and crystal clear
life's beauty will always be near,
if senses fall out of your control
you'll never feel that life is whole.

The smallest things make the world turn
the soft and tender, from them we learn
who we are, without and within
from the source of life
where all things begin.

It makes the most sense
to go the simplest way
diversions may tempt us
for this we will pay.

Some have great wealth
while others have none,
some have good fortune
from wars they have won.

There are those who concede
they take more than they need
only guided by greed
nature's way they don't heed.

Peace of mind that is whole and sound
won't disappear or go away,
while standing firm on solid ground
you can't be fooled or led astray.

Complex things are really one
forming a whole, never undone,
feeling complete is to know nature's power
soaring with knowledge on a stable tower.

A peaceful happy family
is at the heart of a good community,
standing on the bountiful earth
feeling nature's endless worth
reaching what is simply this:
not dwelling in guilt or remiss
just living with a sense of bliss.

A newborn exudes perfect harmony
stinging insects leave it be
and beasts of prey fail to see,
what's soft and small with little strength
with simple thoughts of no great length
pure and wholesome, with tender voice
sensing this world is a place to rejoice.

Remain in harmony with a small child
yet alert as an animal in the wild,
with care in moving, never too quickly
at no time exhausted or becoming sickly,
without struggle nor trying much
keeping a soft and gentle touch.

Those who have lost the way
from all goodness they stray
and themselves betray
unsatisfied 'til their dying day.

Those with knowledge have no need to tell
nor make claims or have a point to sell,
those who tell do not know
talking more they only show
ignorance of nature's flow.

Refined powers of observation
are the source of wisdom's stimulation,
bringing one closer to heaven and earth
while gaining things of true worth.

One who finds this noble path
has no anger, is quick to laugh
has no interest in good or bad
nor deeming a condition sad,
unconcerned with fame or claim
always at peace
without need to blame.

Justice prevails in a peaceful land
with trouble never out of hand
the natural order is simply grand.

Complex laws and bureaucracy
are the seeds of spiritual poverty,
with conflict and weapons yielding war
violent minds making souls poor,
for every rule deftly spoken
another law is often broken.

With common sense we clearly see
the path to righteous liberty:
no force can bring equality
by replacing nature's harmony.

It's best not to insist
how others should live
a dynamic example
is the best way to give.

Happy and sad are not so far apart
and joy never comes from just being smart,
one can't insist or plot and devise
to deny a truth we see with our eyes.

In pursuit of some perfection
don't get lost in one direction,
no need to be callous
when being clear
speak without malice
keep humility near.

To give all that people ask
with single-mindedness,
at its core, a leader's task
from a source quite limitless.

As a mother's love will never cease
as roots will deepen, fruits increase,
a good ruler brings only peace.

Each moment deserves tenderness
with nature's gentle way in mind,
leave no sorrow, no mess
towards suffering don't be blind.

With every good purpose
as with every clear way
creation thrives and blossoms
through the darkest day.

Nature's circle is purely made
with no death or evil to evade.

Everything that holds the most
does so naturally,
the great country, the humble host
find the best things in life are free,
remaining modest
large embracing small
accepting the essence
of one and all.

When the strong submit unto the weak
harmony achieves its highest peak.

Life embraces everything
the wise peasant, the foolish king
heaven above, earth below
infinite space for things to grow,
goodness arrives for one and all
for those who rise and those who fall.

Some acquire much
only wanting more,
most need understanding
having had none before.

Leaders of old knew this to win:
integrity has always been
the source of compassion from within.

Work along with nature's way
calmly fulfilling every day,
life's wholeness has its give and take
be a part of all you make
wary of what might injure you
focused calmly on what you do,
observing the seeming duality
finding simplicity in complexity.

Nature does all work with ease
tasks large and small
brewing storms or a breeze,
without effort, calming rough seas.

Have trust and courage without pride
and difficulties are small and few,
remaining afloat on nature's tide
is a simple and joyful thing to do.

When calmness pervades you can see
how peace prevails quite easily,
before troubles begin and tranquility ends
remain with a stillness that nothing transcends,
to avoid stress or illness and maintain good health
find peace at your core, your greatest true wealth.

A huge tree springs forth from a tiny seed
a long journey starts with one step, indeed.

A stable house has a strong foundation
starting without plans leads to frustration,
a clear focused vision sees a great creation.

Satisfactory results come from pure intent
holding onto what was originally meant,
those who try, and fail to succeed
haven't planned for what they need.

Disappointment emerges from desire
illusive dreams burned up in a fire,
rather find nature's path, follow its way
be part of its cycle, fulfilling each day.

Rulers who are truly wise
fame and fortune, they despise,
they need not prove their cleverness
aware that proud commanders make a mess.

Worthy leaders are wisest, it seems
knowing there isn't a need for extremes,
they simply bring nature's laws within
when the land flourishes, peace can begin.

At the lowest places on Earth
great oceans surge and fill
with all that lakes give forth
and flowing rivers spill,
just as one who quietly and humbly leads
does not use force and yet succeeds.

Demanding leaders, freedoms they take
relying on abuse, all good they forsake,
while a gentle, guiding, even hand
brings a happy, peaceful and flourishing land.

Choose a path infinite and broad
feeling for the suffering,
give what you can afford.

Remain eternal, open-minded and clear
put others ahead without any fear,
with fairness in mind
the world's wealth will appear.

Uncaring and greedy
the conceited will find
they never feel solace
or peace of mind.

Compassion for all
is a heavenly art,
when hearing this call
life will then start.

A show of strength
an angry cry
a raging fight
with tempers high,
these fiery moods get nothing done
nor prove who's right or who has won.

Empathy will never lead you astray
it's the source of joy and nature's way.

Whether dealing with trouble
danger or foe
it is unnecessary
to make any show,
best to retreat and not advance
don't further conflict or rely on chance,
if you encounter problems
it's simple to see
there's no need to struggle
with adversity.

Awareness of the way
means we are prepared
to face the truth
and not be scared.

Nature's way is not complex
naturally, we need to flex.

The rigid find living disconcerting
not caring for others or discerning
what they really should be learning.

The wise find they are wide awake
accomplishing all for nature's sake
knowing that their own fate they make.

Realize it's best to accept and see
the way to do is to be.

Recognizing how little we know
allows us to see and grow,
those who are troubled
thought just before
that they had all the answers
now they know more.

Of discord beware
see distant trouble and care,
before disaster comes near
awaken, remain clear.

Danger not respected
will surely take its toll,
supporting nature's strength
one plays a passive role,
learn to know the inner self
embracing life around
making choices silently
with feet on solid ground.

Someone dies and others live
nature has its take and its give,
at times the world can seem unknown
on difficult days we might feel alone,
these are the moments to become aware
creativity is very much there,
nature connecting everything
with the source of life
and the joy it can bring.

A deadly threat holds its weight
because you care about your fate,
yet knowing the way, one must say:
no one has a right to take life away.

Those who kill
steal unripened fruits
they ignore the way, in dark pursuits,
not knowing compassion
or how to behave
heading to an early grave.

People hunger and often die
if the price of good health is too high,
the sick and hungry surely rebel
when no one assists in making them well.

Death comes to those
burdened and stressed
life is best, when feeling blessed.

In living, we are stretched and flexed
death is rigidity defined,
in stiffness, we remain perplexed
life sustains those with a limber mind.

The dying are those who refuse to change
for nature's course is to re-arrange,
one must keep learning
as life's course keeps turning,
though many find this too strange.

A string brings balance to a bow
as its height shortens, the width will grow
as nature fills the fields we sow.

Most fail to see this natural law
those with much, take even more.

Seeing and balancing nature's wealth
sustaining the living, maintaining good health
finding harmony that we easily share
we lose nothing and become aware
life thrives for those who are generous and fair.

Water simply pervades and yields
seeds absorb it
becoming green fields,
stones may seem
lasting and strong
unbending to water,
they don't last very long.

The hardened have a dismal fate
while the soft and gentle can create
with a focused mind, in a clear state.

Hear the words of sages ringing true:
the humble keep a simple view
with no need to tell others what to do.

Throughout life, flexibility is a must
to understand what's fair and just,
when pliant we learn
respect we earn,
by giving without asking
for something in return.

Yielding is the natural art
accepting change, remaining pure at heart.

The ideal community
is based on natural efficiency,
having only the necessary tools
without punishment or rules,
as deep inside we surely know
what causes us to thrive and grow.

If competing becomes a daily need
the way is lost to greed, indeed.

Strong spices in food and excessive dress
are dispensable, more or less,
if life is full of drama and stress
each day becomes a confusing mess.

An uncomplicated life
has no strife or resentment
by simply finding
calm and contentment.

If there's a need to judge, it's best to wait
for the mind to be in a clear, calm state,
angry discourse can only show
a losing way, a need to grow,
senseless it is to contemplate
how to mold others or manipulate.

Peaceful vision finds problems few
the wise can easily change their view,
anger only clouds the mind
rage in turn, makes you blind,
rather be calm, understanding and kind.

Know anger's source and we can detect
sadness within and then direct
our goodness, towards where we can affect.

Nature's laws are set quite clearly
ignoring them we pay most dearly,
our gentlest thoughts perpetually revive,
the destructive perish, the creative survive.

***

David Marks is a writer, photographer, investigative reporter, documentary filmmaker and horticulturist. He continues to practice Traditional Chinese Medicine.

All of the photos in this book were taken by the author; from the Redwood forest of northern California to the tropical highlands of Central America.

Additional copies of *The Way* can be ordered from your local bookstore or at:

www.laotzu-theway.org